LENIN'S
EMBALMERS

LENIN'S EMBALMERS

A DARK COMEDY
BY VERN THIESSEN

PLAYWRIGHTS CANADA PRESS
TORONTO

PLAYWRIGHTS CANADA PRESS
The Canadian Drama Publisher
215 Spadina Ave., Suite 230, Toronto, ON Canada M5T 2C7
phone 416.703.0013 fax 416.408.3402
info@playwrightscanada.com • www.playwrightscanada.com

Playwrights Canada Press acknowledges the financial support of the Government
of Canada through the Canada Book Fund and the Canada Council for the Arts
and of the Province of Ontario through the Ontario Arts Council and the Ontario
Media Development Corporation for our publishing activities.

 Canada Council Conseil des Arts
for the Arts du Canada
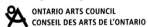 ONTARIO ARTS COUNCIL
CONSEIL DES ARTS DE L'ONTARIO

 Canada Ontario
Ontario Media Development
Corporation

Cover design by Leah Renihan
Type design and layout by Blake Sproule

LIBRARY AND ARCHIVES CANADA CATALOGUING IN PUBLICATION
Thiessen, Vern
Lenin's embalmers / Vern Thiessen.

A play.
Also issued in electronic formats.
ISBN 978-0-88754-970-0

I. Title.

PS8589.H4524L45 2011   C812'.54   C2011-900639-1

First edition: March 2011
Printed and bound in Canada by Hume Intermedia Inc., Scarborough

Mixed Sources

Product group from well-managed forests
and other controlled sources

FSC www.fsc.org Cert no. SGSNA-COC-006478
©1996 Forest Stewardship Council

For my grandfathers, may they rest in peace.

CONTENTS

Lenin's Embalmers was commissioned by the Ensemble Studio Theatre (New York) with the generous assistance of the Alfred P. Sloan Foundation in 2008.

Lenin's Embalmers had its world premiere on March 3, 2010, at the Ensemble Studio Theatre in New York City with the following team:

Lenin	Peter Maloney
Vlad	Zach Grenier
Boris	Scott Sowers
Stalin	Richmond Hoxie
Krasin	Jim Murtagh
Nadia	Polly Lee
Agent 1	Steven Boyer/EJ Cantu
Agent 2	Michael Louis Wells
Director	William Carden
Scenic Design	Mikiko Suzuki MacAdams
Costume Design	Suzanne Chesney
Lighting Design	Chris Dallos
Sound Design	Shane Rettig
Props Design	Meghan Buchanen
Fight Director	J. Allen Suddeth
Stage Manager	Jeff Devolt
Assistant Stage Manager	Michal Mendelson
Assistant Director	Gerritt Turner
Sound Op	Jo Albert
Production Manager	Jack Blacketer
Artistic Director	William Carden
Executive Director	Paul Slee
Associate Artistic Director	Graeme Gillis
Literary Manager	Linsay Firman

Season Producer	Annie Trizna
Marketing	Tim Scales
Intern	Eliza Jane Bowman
Sloan Consultant	Doran Weber
Embalming Consultant	Dorothy Hutchins

Lenin's Embalmers had its Canadian Premiere at the Winnipeg Jewish Theatre (in co-production with the Harold Green Jewish Theatre, Toronto) at the Berney Theatre on October 14, 2010. It opened in Toronto on November 2, 2010, with the following artistic team:

Agent/Ramon	James Durham
Stalin	David Fox
Boris	Martin Julien
Vlad	Hardee Lineham
Agent/Trotsky	Arne MacPherson
Lenin	Harry Nelken
Krasin	Steven Ratzlaff
Nadia	Janine Theriault
Director	Geoffrey Brumlik
Set and Lighting Designers	Guido Tondino & Victoria Zimski
Costume Designer	Janelle Regalbuto
Composer & Sound Designer	Danny Carroll
Stage Manager	Michelle Lagassé
Assistant Stage Manager	Sheena Sanderson
Fight Director	Rick Skene
Production Managers	Rob Rowan & Larry Isacoff
House Technician	Jerry Augustin
Carpenter	Dan Chatham
Props Master	Chris Hadley
Assistant Props Master	Libid Zyla Harder
Lenin Head Manufacturer	Doug Morrow
Wardrobe Assistant	Michelle Cook

Audio Technician	Michael Wright
Scenic Painters	Carla Schroder, Susan Groff, Larry Van Wendt
Running Crew	Jessica Freundl
Production Crew	Alaric Wiens, Drew Derbowka, Ken Perchuk, Ian Phillips

For Winnipeg Jewish Theatre:

Artistic Producer	Michael Nathanson
Associate Producer	Suzie Martin

For Harold Green Theatre

Co-Artistic Directors	David Eisner, Avery Saltzman
General Manager	Matt Birnbaum

PRODUCTION NOTES

I encourage producers to cast the best actors, regardless of gender, age, race or disability.

Non-naturalism in design, acting and directing is encouraged.

With the exception of Nadia, accents of any kind are not to be used.

CHARACTERS

Lenin	A man
Boris	A scientist
Vlad	A scientist
Nadia	She plays Nadias 1, 2 and 3
Stalin	A dictator
Krasin	A man caught in the middle
Agent 1	A secret agent, an apparatchik, a peasant, a student, a prisoner, a guard, Ramon
Agent 2	A secret agent, an apparatchik, a peasant, a student, a prisoner, Trotsky

Ideally, additional actors would be cast to flesh out the world of the play.

ACT ONE

LENIN, alone.

LENIN   Listen to this:

Three Russians are in a Gulag.

No, I'm serious. This is a good one.

Three Russians are in a Gulag.
First Russian says:
What're you in for?
I called Zbarsky a revolutionary, says the second.
That's funny, says the first.
Why? says the second.
I called Zbarsky a *counter*-revolutionary.
That's funny, says the third.
Why? say the others.
I AM Zbarsky.

(a comedian) Uh? Uh?

The ENSEMBLE start to assemble.

You work, you love, you struggle. You become famous, or not. You make a difference, or not. You grow old. Or not. And for what? Why this life? When in the end, you land in the Gulag with everyone else.

(smiles) Me: I could die today.

But I have one more joke to tell.

He collapses into a wheelchair.

***

ENSEMBLE   January.

1924.

We—are Russians.

***

STALIN and KRASIN and TROTSKY.

STALIN   *(to audience)* I—am Stalin.

TROTSKY   *(to audience)* I—am Trotsky.

KRASIN   *(to audience)* I—am Krasin.

STALIN   *(to TROTSKY)* Comrade.

TROTSKY   *(to STALIN)* Comrade.

KRASIN   *(to TROTSKY)* Comrade.

TROTSKY   *(to KRASIN)* Comrade.

STALIN   Comrades: Since the assassination attempt last
               year… *(a look to LENIN)* Comrade Lenin's health
               has grown…

KRASIN   Dire.

STALIN   Dire. So much worse, we fear he will soon be…

KRASIN   No more.

STALIN   No more.

KRASIN   Sadness.

STALIN   Tears.

KRASIN   Grief.

STALIN   We must do something so that the people…

KRASIN   Grow used to him being gone.

TROTSKY   Comrade Nadia is his wife, what does she say to all
               this?

               *LENIN and NADIA 1 separate. LENIN in a wheel-
               chair partially paralyzed. He is desperately finish-
               ing a letter.*

NADIA 1   *(to audience)* I—am Nadia.

LENIN   Nadia!

STALIN   Her view is irrelevant.

NADIA 1	I will soon be the grieving widow.
TROTSKY	She is his wife!
LENIN	Nadia!
NADIA 1	What is it, my love!
STALIN	She is in such a…
KRASIN	Sorrowful…
STALIN	In such a sorrowful state…
LENIN	I am dying.
NADIA 1	Oh Ilyich!
KRASIN	She cannot see…
STALIN	She cannot see the bigger picture.
NADIA 1	Let me rub your hands.
STALIN	We must consider what is to be done.
LENIN	Write this down:

He dictates. She writes.

TROTSKY	Cremation is best.
KRASIN	Cremation?
STALIN	A Russian?
KRASIN	Unthinkable.

LENIN   I want no grave.

TROTSKY   No grave.

LENIN   No monuments.

TROTSKY   No monuments.

LENIN   No shrines.

TROTSKY   No shrines.

KRASIN   No.

STALIN   No, but…

TROTSKY   What.

STALIN   We understand our comrade scientists…

KRASIN   Our comrade scientists…

STALIN   In the provinces…

KRASIN   Are…

STALIN   Are now able to…

KRASIN   Preserve.

TROTSKY   "Preserve"?

STALIN   Preserve a body.

KRASIN   A body…

STALIN   Preserve a body for a considerable—

KRASIN   A considerable—

STALIN   *(to KRASIN)* Be quiet or I will kill you.

           Pause.

TROTSKY   How long?

STALIN   A CONSIDERABLE. Amount. Of time.

TROTSKY   And who ARE these comrade scientists in the provinces?

KRASIN   None of your—

STALIN   *(to TROTSKY)* None of your concern.

TROTSKY   Comrade Stalin, do you intend to replace the bones
           of the saints with the body of Lenin?

STALIN   Of course not.

KRASIN   Of course not.

TROTSKY   Because if you are, you are betraying Lenin, you are
           betraying his ideals, you are betraying this country.

LENIN   And don't let that ignoramus Stalin take over. Trotsky
           is the future.

           NADIA 1 hands the letter back and helps him sign.

TROTSKY   Vladimir Ilyich is not yet dead, and his TRUE suc-
           cessor not yet chosen. Remember that—comrade.

           STALIN, a monster in his eyes.

STALIN   Are... you... THREATENING me?

Stalin rises. Lenin has a stroke.

LENIN   Nadia!

              He can no longer speak.

NADIA 1   Ilyich!? I'll get the doctor.

STALIN   ARE YOU?

NADIA 1   Ilyich! Don't leave me, don't…

              She runs off. Trotsky smirks.

STALIN   Now if there's nothing else…

TROTSKY   Comrades. Do we know who tried to kill Comrade
              Lenin?

KRASIN   The VaCheka are investigating.

TROTSKY   The who?

STALIN   The All-Russian Extraordinary Commission for
              Combating Counter-Revolution and Sabotage.

KRASIN   The secret police.

TROTSKY   WHAT secret police?

STALIN   The one I created.

TROTSKY   When?

STALIN   This morning.

KRASIN   It was in all the papers.

STALIN	Didn't you see?
TROTSKY	And will they find out who did it?
STALIN	Of course.
KRASIN	Of course.

STALIN takes the letter from LENIN and crumples it up.

STALIN	People can't go around shooting whomever they want. *(a smirk)* Can they?
TROTSKY	*(to audience)* It was then—that I fled.
LENIN	*(to audience)* It was then—that I died.

***

VLAD	*(to audience)* I am Vladimir.
BORIS	*(to audience)* I am Boris.
VLAD	*(to audience)* I am the hero of this story.
BORIS	*(to audience)* *I* am the hero of this story.
VLAD	YOU GO AWAY!

BORIS hesitates.

NOW!

BORIS leaves.

VLAD takes a shot of vodka.

***

A lecture hall in the provinces.

VLAD   Today's lecture will look at the preservation of tissue. Slide!

             Slide.

             The study of biological cells is the new frontier. Although preserving tissue is not a modern practice, the scientific understanding of it is relatively unknown. In ancient times—

             KRASIN bursts in with APPARATCHIK 1 and APPARATCHIK 2, who is drunk.

             They are very aware of the class.

KRASIN   Professor Vorobiov.

VLAD   Excuse me!

KRASIN   We are the Soviet Committee for Immortalization.

VLAD   Immortalization of whom?

KRASIN   Whomever we…

APPARAT 1   …Feel needs…

APPARAT 2   Immortalizing.

VLAD   I am in the middle of a lecture.

APPARAT 1   Exactly why we're here.

APPARAT 2   Exactly.

KRASIN   We have travelled.

APPARAT 1   A great distance.

APPARAT 2   From Moscow!

KRASIN   To here.

APPARAT 1   The provinces.

APPARAT 2   To listen.

KRASIN   To you.

APPARAT 1   Please.

APPARAT 2   Continue.

KRASIN   Speak.

            VLAD carries on.

VLAD   …The practices of various cultures are worth exam-
             ining as they relate to modern science. Slide!

            Slide.

             In ancient Rome, for example, mourners wrapped the
             body of the deceased in wax, aromatic salt, honey and
             balsam before placing him in—

            APPARATCHIK 1 raises his hand.

             Yes?

APPARAT 1   *(hits 2)* Go!

APPARAT 2   What?

APPARAT 1   *(to 2)* Steeping!

APPARAT 2   Huh?

APPARAT 1   *(to 2)* The tissue!

APPARAT 2   The…?

KRASIN   *(to VLAD)* Once the body has been—

VLAD   The body of what?

KRASIN   *(oops)* …Let's say the "body" of…

APPARAT 1   "A Man."

APPARAT 2   "A Man," yes!

KRASIN   If the tissues of "A Man…"

APPARAT 2   If the tissues of a man…

APPARAT 1   Were STEEPED in glycerin…

APPARAT 2   Would they not be preserved for a, a, an eternity?

VLAD   An interesting theory…

APPARAT 2   Ah ha!

VLAD   But no.

APPARAT 2   No?

VLAD	That procedure can only be applied to certain parts of the body: the head, the arms, the legs. But the internal organs must be treated separately and kept in their own containers.
APPARAT 2	Damn!
APPARAT 1	But nitrogen!
VLAD	Nitrogen?
APPARAT 1	Liquid nitrogen creates a lower storage temperature than glycerin.
VLAD	But nitrogen does NOT prevent the appearance of anaerobic microbes. The preservation may last, but not without outward signs of decay.
APPARAT 2	You see?
KRASIN	But refrigeration!
VLAD	Refrigeration?
KRASIN	*(excited)* Once the body is frozen and the tissues fixed with formalin—the enzymes causing autolysis will become inactive and prevent bacteria.
VLAD	It is true temperatures of -100 °C are necessary for prolonged storage of biological materials.
KRASIN	AH HA!
VLAD	BUT! The formalin solution he speaks of will, in fact, ACCELERATE the process of deterioration.
APPARAT 1	*(snicker)* You see?

APPARAT 2	*(snicker)* See?
KRASIN	*(steamed)* Are you telling us, professor, that the long-term conservation of a body is impossible?
VLAD	Not at all.
	He shows specimens in jars: heart, lung, brain.
	How old do you think these are?
KRASIN	A month?
VLAD	Older.
APPARAT 1	A year.
VLAD	Older.
APPARAT 2	This one looks REALLY good!
VLAD	Twenty years.
KRASIN	Impossible!
VLAD	Twenty years they have been sitting in my office. And they look as good as when I first embalmed them.
KRASIN	How?
APPARAT 1	Tell us!
APPARAT 2	Tell!
VLAD	That, my dear committee, is a secret I will carry to my grave.

KRASIN	You could be fired.
VLAD	I still have my secret.
APPARAT 1	You could be sent to the Gulag.
VLAD	I still have my secret.
APPARAT 2	You could be…

He mimes a gunshot to the head.

VLAD	*(steaming)* I am a man of science. And I won't be threatened in my own lecture hall. Now all of you. Go back to Moscow. GO!

***

BORIS	*(to audience)* I am Boris.
VLAD	*(to audience)* I am Vladimir.
NADIA 2	*(to audience)* I am Nadia. But not the same Nadia as before.
BORIS	I am the *real* hero of this story.
NADIA 2	I will now be the unhappy wife.
VLAD	I tell you *I* am the real hero!
BORIS	*(to VLAD)* YOU go away!

VLAD leaves.

***

Boris's apartment.

Drip. Drip.

Boris is writing.

It's cold.

NADIA 2   There's a hole in the ceiling.

BORIS   I know.

NADIA 2   There is dripping.

BORIS   I hear.

NADIA 2   There is water dripping from the hole in the ceiling.

BORIS   Logic.

NADIA 2   It's cold.

BORIS   Wear another sweater.

NADIA 2   I only HAVE one sweater.

BORIS   Warm the oven.

NADIA 2   We need the wood.

BORIS   Go to bed.

NADIA 2   It's full of bugs.

BORIS   Eat something.

NADIA 2   Stale bread and mouldy potatoes and rotting meat—

BORIS   BE QUIET, THEN!

            Drip. Drip.

NADIA 2   We can't live like this.

BORIS   There's no other choice.

NADIA 2   You must find work.

BORIS   What do you think I am doing?

NADIA 2   What is it?

BORIS   A position—at the university.

NADIA 2   Ha!

BORIS   What?

NADIA 2   Ha ha!

BORIS   You complain and then you mock, you MOCK!

NADIA 2   They'll never give it to a Jew.

BORIS   They gave me the head of the chemical plant.

NADIA 2   That was in SIBERIA.

BORIS   Well you LOVED Siberia, didn't you? You thought it
            was WONDERFUL. What, with your maids and horses
            and LOVERS and good food and horses and LOVERS
            and maids and good food and HORSES—

NADIA 2   You should have worked harder.

BORIS   They shut down the factory.

NADIA 2   You should have stayed longer.

BORIS   I am not going to spend my life slaving away in the provinces.

NADIA 2   You should have opened a hat shop.

BORIS   There was a WAR.

NADIA 2   Everyone can use a hat.

BORIS   A REVOLUTION.

NADIA 2   Who can't use another hat?

BORIS   And an ECONOMIC CRISIS!

NADIA 2   I AM DEPRESSED, THIS IS DEPRESSING, YOU ARE DEPRESSING ME!

Knock, knock.

Don't answer.

BORIS   Why?

NADIA 2   'Cause if you do, and it's bad, you'll die.

Knock, knock.

BORIS   But if I don't answer, and it's bad…

NADIA 2   You'll die.

Knock, knock.

BORIS	I'll answer.
NADIA 2	Boris!
BORIS	It could be an opportunity.

Knock, knock.

Who's there?

The AGENTS burst in.

AGENT 1	Boris Zbarsky?
BORIS	Perhaps.
AGENT 2	Nadia Zbarsky?
NADIA 2	Who wants to know?
AGENT 1	We're from the VaCheka.
NADIA 2	The who?
AGENT 2	The All-Russian Extraordinary Commission for Combating Counter-Revolution and Sabotage.
AGENT 1	The secret police.
AGENT 2	Come with us.
BORIS	Where?
AGENT 1	None of your concern.
BORIS	Why?

AGENT 2	None of your concern.
NADIA 2	Wait!

She holds vodka.

A bottle each?

They consider.

Surely that will buy us all some… time?

They sit. NADIA 2 pours for all.

ALL	*Nazdarovya.*

They all down it in unison.

BORIS	So.
AGENT 1	So.
BORIS	So.
AGENT 2	We're taking you with us.
BORIS	Where?
AGENT 1	The Kremlin.
BORIS	Why?
AGENT 2	Lenin is dead.
NADIA 2	*(a gasp)*

They all drink.

BORIS   Why me?

AGENT 2   You know Krasin.

BORIS   He got me the position in Siberia.

AGENT 1   He says you know about chemicals.

AGENT 2   He says you're the perfect person.

BORIS   For what?

AGENT 1   To help.

BORIS   With what?

AGENT 1   The body.

NADIA 2   *(a gasp)*

                They all drink.

BORIS   Who would agree to even TRY such a thing?

AGENT 2   Someone who wants to…

AGENT 1   Serve Mother Russia.

AGENT 2   And help Her People

AGENT 1   And do a Great Service.

NADIA 2   And have a good house?

                They look at her.

AGENT 1   Perhaps.

NADIA 2   And a good position?

AGENT 1   Perhaps.

NADIA 2   And a lot of money?

AGENT 2   Perhaps.

NADIA 2   Even though they were a Jew?

AGENT 2   Even better.

BORIS   Why?

AGENT 1   If a Jew fails…

AGENT 2   Twice as easy to kill.

The agents laugh.

***

KRASIN   Borislav Gerhardovich.

BORIS   Alexander Petrolovich.

KRASIN   How is our dear Nadia?

BORIS   Oy.

KRASIN   A difficult time.

BORIS   Sasha my friend, I need a position.

KRASIN   And I need you.

He pulls up a sheet on a table.

Boris is struck. The smell of death.

BORIS   What happened?

KRASIN   Stroke. Perhaps brought on by the lodged bullet.

BORIS   How long has he…?

KRASIN   A week. And he's already showing signs of decomposition. Look: the skin on his face and hands—they've darkened. Wrinkles on his torso and arms. His lips starting to part.

BORIS   What are you going to do?

KRASIN   Stalin wants him embalmed.

BORIS   How long?

KRASIN   Forever.

BORIS   You're joking.

KRASIN   Am I laughing?

BORIS   For a week, yes. For a month, maybe. But an eternity?

KRASIN   Can you do it?

BORIS   Not me.

KRASIN   Then who?

BORIS   No one. Except…

He hesitates.

KRASIN   Who?

BORIS   Vladimir Vorobiov.

KRASIN   No!

BORIS   Why?

KRASIN   He's a Jew.

BORIS   I'm a Jew.

KRASIN   He's an enemy of Mother Russia.

BORIS   Please.

KRASIN   I went ALL THE WAY TO THE PROVINCES and he
                called me an IDIOT! ME! Do you know what it's
                like in the provinces? Everywhere you look, noth-
                ing but STEPPES. Freezing is the best method.

BORIS   Freezing? Look: bring him to Moscow.

KRASIN   No.

BORIS   Let him see the body.

KRASIN   No.

BORIS   Do you have a choice?

                Silence.

                Let me talk to him.
                I've known him a long time.
                I know what makes him tick.
                Besides, we need him.

KRASIN   We?

BORIS   If I convince him, surely I'll be… thanked?

KRASIN   Don't fail me, Borislav Gerhardovich. Or we'll BOTH
              be on our way to the Gulag.

              They look at LENIN.

BORIS   We'll need to do something. Until he gets here.

KRASIN   I still think freezing—

BORIS   NO!

KRASIN   ALL RIGHT! Whatever you suggest.

              They lift the sheet.

              LENIN *jumps from the table.*

              Amazing.

LENIN   Here's a good one.

BORIS   The Father of the Revolution.

LENIN   Stalin and Trotsky are having tea.

KRASIN   He looks at peace.

BORIS   Shame he'll never see it.

                            ***

LENIN   Stalin and Trotsky are having tea.

TROTSKY   Comrade Stalin.

LENIN   Says Trotsky.

TROTSKY   What is the difference between capitalism and socialism?

STALIN   In a capitalist society man exploits man.

LENIN   Says Stalin.

TROTSKY   And in socialism?

STALIN   It's the other way around.

            TROTSKY and LENIN laugh.

TROTSKY   Very good, comrade, very…

            STALIN does not laugh.

LENIN   There's a saying: Those who can't laugh—can't lead.

                            ***

            VLAD's office in the provinces.

VLAD   *(to audience)* I am Vladimir—as you might recall.

NADIA 3   *(to audience)* I am Nadia—but not the same Nadia
            as before.

VLAD   *(shy)* Hello.

NADIA 3   *(shy)* Hello.

VLAD   *(to audience)* This is my office—in the provinces.

NADIA 3 *(to audience)* I am now the brilliant—yet shy—scientist.

VLAD *(to audience)* I've always been shy around women named Nadia.

NADIA 3 *(to audience)* Every woman in this story is called Nadia.

VLAD Drink?

NADIA 3 I…

VLAD A wee one?

NADIA 3 If you insist.

VLAD Nazdarovya.

> *He downs it, nervous. She sips.*

> This is where I study.

NADIA 3 Yes.

VLAD This is where I… experiment.

NADIA 3 Yes.

VLAD I am looking for a secretary.

NADIA 3 Hm.

VLAD You are looking for work.

NADIA 3 Yes.

VLAD And what is your experience? Don't answer! I don't want to know.

NADIA 3   I am interested. In science.

VLAD   Are you?

NADIA 3   Very.

VLAD   Well then.

      He shows the specimens.

      Observe: a heart. The lung. The brain. So young, this woman, so…

      He looks at NADIA 3.

      Like you. And I…

      He approaches her.

      I like to keep things young.

      He reaches out his hand, gently.

      Forever.

      The AGENTS burst in.

AGENTS   Vladimir Vorobiov?

VLAD   Who are you?

AGENT 2   We're from the Unified State Political Administration.

VLAD   You mean the VaCheka?

AGENT 1   They changed the name.

VLAD   When?

AGENT 1   This morning.

AGENT 2   It was in all the papers.

AGENT 1   Didn't you see?

AGENT 2   Come with us.

VLAD   Where?

AGENT 1   None of your concern.

VLAD   Why?

AGENT 2   None of your concern.

NADIA 3   Wait!

                She holds vodka.

                A bottle of the finest?

                They consider.

                Surely that will buy us all some… time?

                They sit. NADIA 3 pours for all.

ALL   Nazdarovya.

                They all down it in unison.

VLAD   So.

AGENT 1   So.

VLAD   So.

AGENT 2   We're taking you to Moscow.

VLAD   Where?

AGENT 1   The Kremlin.

VLAD   Why?

AGENT 2   Lenin is dead.

NADIA 3   *(a gasp)*

              Drink.

VLAD   Why me?

AGENT 1   You know Zbarsky.

VLAD   Zbarsky? What's he got to do with this?

AGENT 2   He says you know about chemicals.

AGENT 1   He says you're the perfect person.

VLAD   For what?

AGENT 1   To help.

VLAD   With what?

AGENT 2   The body.

NADIA 3   *(a gasp)*

              Drink.

VLAD   Who would agree to even TRY such a thing?

AGENT 2   Someone who wants to…

AGENT 1   Serve Mother Russia.

AGENT 2   And help Her People.

AGENT 1   And do a Great Service.

NADIA 3   *(tipsy)* And have a better lab?

            They look at her.

AGENT 1   Perhaps.

NADIA 3   And a promotion?

AGENT 2   Perhaps.

NADIA 3   And a personal assistant?

AGENT 2   Everything is possible.

AGENT 1   *(toast)* In Moscow.

NADIA 3   *(toast)* Moscow.

AGENTS   *(toast)* Moscow.

            They drink.

                        ***

            Moscow.

They all surround LENIN's body.

VLAD replaces the sheet.

NADIA 3 gives him a cloth to wipe his hands.

KRASIN, BORIS, APPARATCHIK 1 and 2 watch.

Horrible expectation.

Finally, VLAD faces them.

VLAD   Impossible.

                A burst, overlap:

KRASIN   What?

APPARAT 1   My god!

APPARAT 2   What'd he say?!

VLAD   It's too late.

KRASIN   Look here, "Professor"!

VLAD   His lips are three centimetres apart, there are brown
                patches on his thighs, his left hand is turning grey, his
                ears are crumpling and his BRAIN has been removed.

APPARAT 1   It is being studied!

APPARAT 2   For brilliance!

VLAD   Bury him and be done with it.

APPARAT 1   We must try nitrogen before it's too late!

APPARAT 2	Glycerin!
APPARAT 1	Nitrogen!
APPARAT 2	Glycerin!

They rush out arguing.

KRASIN	*(to VLAD)* Have a safe trip back to the STEPPE!
BORIS	Wait.
KRASIN	I TOLD you.
BORIS	Sasha…
KRASIN	I took a risk, a very big risk.
BORIS	I haven't even had a chance to talk to him. Give me a day. One day.
KRASIN	One day. After that? We FREEZE him!

He leaves.

VLAD is packing up.

BORIS	*(warm)* Vladimir Davidovich.
VLAD	*(cool)* Borislav Gerhardovich.
BORIS	How many years has it been?
VLAD	I haven't been counting.
BORIS	I hear you're making breakthroughs, out there, in the provinces.

VLAD	I'm only doing what you never have.
BORIS	What's that?
VLAD	Work hard. Did YOU do this?
BORIS	What?
VLAD	Whatever's been injected into the body.
BORIS	It's standard: formalin, alcohol, glycerin.
VLAD	The solution has leaked.
BORIS	And what should I have done?
VLAD	A better job.
BORIS	*(to NADIA 3)* He hasn't changed.
VLAD	Neither have you.
BORIS	Always suffering.
VLAD	Always lazy.
BORIS	Everything impossible.
VLAD	Everything half-baked.
BORIS	Never happy.
VLAD	But never a traitor.

BORIS looks at him.

Tension.

I have to go.

BORIS   Wait, wait…

        BORIS has dug out a bottle and two shot glasses.

        A moment of your time. Old friend. In… private?

        VLAD hesitates, but can't resist the booze.

VLAD   *(to NADIA 3)* I won't be long.

        She leaves.

        BORIS pours.

        They shoot it back.

        BORIS pours another.

        They drink throughout.

BORIS   Pretty.

VLAD   Yes.

BORIS   You always did have a weakness for beautiful women.

VLAD   It's not weakness, it's TASTE.

BORIS   Of course.

        BORIS pours. They drink.

        It's good to see you.

VLAD   Is it.

BORIS   You're looking well.

VLAD   Don't flatter me, Boris. Just tell me what you want.

             BORIS pours, they drink.

BORIS   We have an opportunity here.

VLAD   Yes… for a FIRING SQUAD.

BORIS   There must be a way.

VLAD   You know what happened to the men who tried to embalm Pope Alexander VI?

BORIS   Sainthood?

VLAD   Tortured. Hanged and quartered. In public.

BORIS   This is different.

VLAD   Is it.

BORIS   This is science.

VLAD   This isn't science, this is politics.

BORIS   You handle the science, I handle the politics.

VLAD   And you've handled things so well in the past.

BORIS   Forget the past. We both want the same thing.

VLAD   Is that so.

BORIS   Recognition.

VLAD	Ha!
BORIS	Success.
VLAD	Ha!
BORIS	Wealth!
VLAD	No, those are things YOU want.
BORIS	What, your dream is a measly part-time job in the provinces?
VLAD	I LIKE the provinces.
BORIS	Do you.
VLAD	They house me.
BORIS	In a slum.
VLAD	I dine out every night.
BORIS	On turnip soup.
VLAD	Vodka is cheap.
BORIS	Vodka is cheap everywhere. You want better, I know you do.
VLAD	It's too risky.
BORIS	We could be the first.
VLAD	It's too dangerous.
BORIS	"Two Jews Embalm Lenin."

VLAD   "Two Jews Die In Salt Mine."

BORIS   We'll be famous, we'll be HEROES!

VLAD   No.
               No, "old friend."
               We'll be dead.

               He downs the shot.

               Goodbye, Borislav Gerhardovich.

               BORIS stops him.

BORIS   You have to do this.

VLAD   No I don't.

BORIS   Yes. You do.

VLAD   What are you saying?

               Silence.

               What?

               VLAD grabs BORIS roughly.

               WHAT ARE YOU SAYING!?

BORIS   THE TSAR!

VLAD   Don't. You. Even. DARE.

BORIS   You loved the tsar.

VLAD   And you loved TROTSKY!

BORIS   The tsar killed thousands of Jews.

VLAD   So did the revolution.

BORIS   If there wasn't a revolution—

VLAD   If there wasn't a revolution, we wouldn't be HERE staring at Lenin's body.

BORIS   Trotsky is our only hope.

VLAD   Trotsky has no loyalties. He was against the tsar, then he was against Stalin, then he was against Lenin, then he was FOR Lenin, then he was FOR Stalin, now he's AGAINST Stalin. He's a traitor!

BORIS   No! YOU are the traitor!

A fight.

Very Russian: dirty, tragic, ridiculous.

Snake!

VLAD   Parasite!

BORIS   Mad Dog!

VLAD   Rabid Wolf!

BORIS   Fascist hyena!

VLAD   Dogmatist pig!

BORIS   Lumpen proletariat!

VLAD   Rootless cosmopolitan!

BORIS   Yoke of capitalist exploitation!

VLAD   *Petit-bourgeois* nationalist!

BORIS   If Stalin finds out you sided with the tsar—

VLAD   If Stalin finds out you sided with Trotsky—

BORIS   You are doomed.

VLAD   No, YOU are doomed.

BORIS   ENOUGH!

They part. On the floor panting.

VLAD   You stole my work.

BORIS   It was OURS.

VLAD   You took our research and published it under YOUR NAME.

BORIS   I had to do it.

VLAD   If it hadn't been for me—

BORIS   It was the only way we could survive!

VLAD   You never gave me credit for ANYTHING. And now look at you. Flattering me. Threatening me. Begging me. You're nothing but a desperate little WORM.

BORIS   You're right. I AM desperate. But there's something in this for you too.

I am trying to GIVE you something, Vlad. I am trying to pay you BACK.

I am trying to make things RIGHT. Let go of the past, and see what a great chance this is. You get what you've always wanted, what you deserve.

VLAD   And that is?

BORIS   Respect.

The word a dart in VLAD's heart.

He thinks.

Then:

VLAD   I want the credit, if we're not killed.

BORIS   Of course.

VLAD   I want the honours, if we're not executed.

BORIS   Yes, yes.

VLAD   I mean it!

BORIS   Whatever you want.

VLAD   A full position. At the university.

BORIS   …All right.

VLAD   And the best lab equipment.

BORIS   Fine.

VLAD   And I want… an assistant.

BORIS   You mean…? *(the girl?)*

VLAD   Yes.

BORIS   I'll see what I can do.

              Now. What about the body?

VLAD   Oy…

              VLAD grabs the bottle, pours.

              Even if it were in perfect condition…

BORIS   What can we do?

              VLAD hesitates.

              Tell me.

VLAD   We need time. To experiment. Carefully.

BORIS   How long?

VLAD   I don't know. A few months at least.

BORIS   What else?

              BORIS gets out pen and paper. He writes it down.

VLAD   Controlled temperatures.

BORIS   You mean…?

VLAD   Cold conditions at first, but then…

BORIS   Could we do it underground?

VLAD   The permafrost is six feet deep!

BORIS   So dynamite the site.

VLAD   Ha!

BORIS   I'm serious. They can build the mausoleum above us.

VLAD   But we still need to control the temperature.

BORIS   Stoves.

VLAD   Stoves?! They'll never do any of this, Boris.

BORIS   They will. If they want it, they'll give us anything.
             Keep going.

             Pause.

VLAD   A staff.

BORIS   For…?

VLAD   Documentation, preparing the chemicals, monitor-
             ing the body.

BORIS   Next.

VLAD   A large bath. To immerse him.

BORIS   Metal?

VLAD   No. It will react with the chemicals.

BORIS   Rubber.

VLAD   If it's made to our specifications.

BORIS   Go on.

VLAD   A sarcophagus.

BORIS   Easy enough.

VLAD   But of glass. Like the jars I use for my specimens.

BORIS   Done.

VLAD   If we can get all that, we may stand a chance of embalming him properly.

BORIS   Excellent.

VLAD   And if we re-embalm him every six months or so…

BORIS   Every six months?

VLAD   How else do you think he's going to last an eternity? Not even the ancient Egyptians solved that.

BORIS   So, we, we have to…?

VLAD   Re-embalm Lenin every six months, yes.

                BORIS sees a pot of gold.

                Perhaps he does a little dance.

BORIS   *(ecstatic)* A job for life!

                Here. Sign this.

                BORIS reads aloud as VLAD scans it:

> Dear Comrades. The body's condition is worsening by the day. The only way to save the body is by giving me everything I want. My needs are attached. Vladimir Vorobiov.

VLAD   This is insane.

BORIS   No, Vlad. To keep the dream of the revolution alive, they must keep Lenin alive. Forever. And you—we—are the only ones who can do that.

VLAD   Why do I feel like I have a gun to my head?

BORIS   Trust me.

> *VLAD signs.*

***

> *KRASIN and BORIS.*

BORIS   We are ready to save the body.

KRASIN   We, who's we?

BORIS   Vorobiov and myself.

KRASIN   *(scoffs)* Ha!

BORIS   Here is a note detailing his needs.

KRASIN   "Everything I want"?

BORIS   It's not *my* suggestion.

KRASIN   Whose is it?

BORIS   Yours.

              BORIS smiles. KRASIN gets it.

KRASIN   You better know what you're doing.

BORIS   One more thing.

KRASIN   What.

BORIS   The fee.

KRASIN   Well?

BORIS   Twenty-five.

KRASIN   Twenty-five hundred rubles? Are you mad?

BORIS   Twenty-five THOUSAND.

              KRASIN is dumbstruck.

              Each.

                            ***

              STALIN and KRASIN.

STALIN   I received the note.

KRASIN   Yes?

STALIN   We should…

KRASIN   We should…?

STALIN   Try it?

KRASIN	Try it?
STALIN	No?
KRASIN	No, I mean—
STALIN	I'm glad you agree.
KRASIN	Yes.
STALIN	We will make Lenin live forever.
KRASIN	Yes.
STALIN	We will immortalize communism for all time.
KRASIN	Yes.
STALIN	We will replace the cathedral with a mausoleum. We will construct a new faith. Where is Trotsky?
KRASIN	In hiding.
STALIN	I KNOW that, but WHERE!?
KRASIN	No one knows.
STALIN	No one knows?
	Take a note:
	"Memo: To all secret agents worldwide: Find Trotsky. Or I will kill you. Your leader. Stalin."
	Get the embalmers started.

KRASIN   What if… they fail.

STALIN   Fail?

KRASIN   I only meant… that… we can always bury Lenin.

STALIN   If they fail, they will be shot. THEN we bury Lenin.

                                    ***

                BORIS with clipboard and pen.

                VLAD with vodka.

BORIS   Vlad!

VLAD   What!?

BORIS   We start in three days! I need to write it down.

VLAD   I know what I'm doing.

BORIS   But I don't. We need to figure out WHAT we're going
                to do, HOW we're going to do it, and the SUPPLIES
                we're going to need.

                VLAD drinks.

                BORIS takes the booze away.

                Hey! Give me that back!

                Not until we're finished. Now tell me.

                VLAD relents.

VLAD   We remove the sutures from the head and chest.

BORIS   Hang on, hang on.

BORIS writes.

VLAD   Next: we remove lungs, liver, spleen.

BORIS   Slow down, slow down.

VLAD   Then: we flush the rib cage.

BORIS   With what?

VLAD   Distilled water. And we fix the tissues with formalin.

BORIS   What about the body and face?

VLAD   Wads of wool steeped in one percent solution of formaldehyde.

BORIS   And the cavity?

VLAD   Acetic acid.

BORIS   Got it. Then?

VLAD   We raise the temperature to minus ten degrees using the stoves.

BORIS   What if we can't?

VLAD   What?

BORIS   What happens if we can't control the temperature?

VLAD   The body won't take the solution.

BORIS   And so then what do we do?

VLAD   Well, in that case, we SHOOT ourselves, that's what we do.

BORIS   Vlad!

VLAD   I don't know!

BORIS   You don't KNOW?

VLAD   There's only so much we can prepare.

BORIS   We cannot make a mistake.

VLAD   I know.

BORIS   We only have one chance to get this right.

VLAD   I know.

BORIS   If we fail—

VLAD   This has never been DONE before, remember?!

         Pause.

         We immerse the body anyway.

BORIS   And if the body still doesn't absorb the formula?

VLAD   We hang ourselves.

BORIS   Grrr!

VLAD   You hang me, and I'll—no, that doesn't work.

BORIS   VLAD.

VLAD   We, we, we up the solution.

BORIS	To what?
VLAD	Three percent formaldehyde.
BORIS	Three percent?! Do you realize—!?
VLAD	I know.
BORIS	That's toxic!
VLAD	I know.
BORIS	We could DIE!
VLAD	Do you have a better idea?

Silence.

And if THAT doesn't work, we…

BORIS	We…?
VLAD	We give up.

VLAD is stumped. BORIS is thinking.

BORIS	We cut.
VLAD	What?
BORIS	The body.
VLAD	Cut the body of LENIN?
BORIS	Small cuts.
VLAD	And where do you plan to make these small cuts?

BORIS	The armpits. The webbing of the fingers. The abdomen.
	Where the public won't see them.
VLAD	Huh. And if the body still doesn't absorb the solution?
BORIS	Add alcohol.
VLAD	How much?
BORIS	Twenty percent.
VLAD	How long?
BORIS	A week, ten days. And if we mix it with glycerin…
VLAD	It will help the skin colour.
BORIS	And create better elasticity, yes?
VLAD	Yes, yes! But the question remains:
	What if the body still doesn't absorb the solution? What then?
	Silence. They think.
	Then, a discovery:
	…Potassium acetate.
BORIS	No, no.
VLAD	Why.
BORIS	It will react badly with the formalin.

VLAD	No no, just the opposite. The nature of potassium acetate is...?
BORIS	Highly hygroscopic!
VLAD	Exactly, it retains water.
BORIS	So then we...?
VLAD	Keep adding more potassium acetate until the tissues absorb it.
BORIS	Brilliant!

BORIS writes.

VLAD	And then what?
BORIS	The face. It's a mess.
VLAD	Acetic acid?
BORIS	But diluted in water, yes?
VLAD	Yes, it will soften the wrinkles.
BORIS	Plus a small percentage of hydrogen peroxide to restore the original colouring.
VLAD	And carbolic acid to deal with the damp spots.
BORIS	Excellent. And the mouth?
VLAD	Oy!
BORIS	Stitches.

VLAD   Stitches?

BORIS   Very fine thread. Under the mustache to close the
                lips.

VLAD   Good!

BORIS   But the eyes, they're so sunken…

VLAD   Replace them with false ones.

BORIS   Won't people notice?

VLAD   Not once you've sewn them shut?

                BORIS smiles. Then he writes:

BORIS   So, over four months, we need…?

VLAD   Two hundred litres of glycerin, I would think.

BORIS   Fifty kilos of potassium acetate.

VLAD   Make it a hundred.

BORIS   One hundred kilos of potassium…

VLAD   Fifteen hundred litres of water.

BORIS   Disinfectant?

VLAD   Say three hundred litres to be safe.

BORIS   And fifty litres quinine chloride, one percent?

VLAD   Good.

Boris adds it up.

BORIS   Not cheap.

VLAD   No?

BORIS   No. But when we're done, he will look…

VLAD   Yes. It will be…

BORIS   Yes. Yes, it will. Yes.

They smile at each other.

Boris pours them shots.

Step one.

VLAD   Remove sutures from head and chest.

***

Boris is packing.

NADIA 2   Where are you going?

BORIS   I can't tell you.

NADIA 2   Are you leaving me?

BORIS   No.

NADIA 2   Do you have a LOVER?

BORIS   No!

I'll be back in a few months.

NADIA 2   Is it important?

BORIS   Yes.

NADIA 2   Will it make me happy?

BORIS   Yes.

NADIA 2   Will we be rich?

BORIS   Perhaps.

NADIA 2   Is it dangerous?

BORIS   *(sexy)* In a way.

NADIA 2   Will you die?

BORIS   I hope not.

NADIA 2   Can I take a lover while you're gone?

BORIS   No.

NADIA 2   Please?

BORIS   No!

NADIA 2   What's this?

BORIS   Ah! It's my… journal.

            She runs off with it, playful. He chases.

NADIA 2   Can I read it?

BORIS   No!

He catches her. She gives it back.

Behave yourself while I'm gone.

He finishes packing.

Now wish me luck.

A kiss.

NADIA 2   Luck.

***

LENIN stands in the quintessential pose: one hand pointing out, the other in his upper chest pocket.

LENIN   Two peasants are in a square.

Two PEASANTS enter.

They come upon a statue of me, in my classic pose.

PEASANT 1   Why do they always show him standing like that?

LENIN   Says the one.

PEASANT 2   I'll tell you.

LENIN   Says the second.

PEASANT 2   One hand proclaims: All this land is yours.

PEASANT 1   And the other?

LENIN pulls a fist full of rubles out of his pocket.

PEASANT 2   All your money is mine!

                   *The PEASANTS laugh and leave. STALIN wanders
                   on.*

LENIN   Want to live? They kill you.
                   Want to die? They won't let you.
                   Want to be forgotten? They build a statue of you.
                   Want to leave something behind?

                   He looks at STALIN.

They EMBALM you.

                   LENIN remains, watches during the following.

                              ***

                   An explosion.

                   Then: the floor slowly sinks.

                   A cellar unearthed, as if a grave.

                   Breath swirls, as if a spirit.

                   Technicians active, as if maggots.

                   VLAD and BORIS roll in a table.

                   LENIN revealed, his body a wreckage.

                   As VLAD speaks the technicians take photos.

                   NADIA 3 is taking notes for VLAD.

VLAD	Corpse has turned sallow. Marked discolouration around the eyes, nose, ears and temples.

NADIA 3 takes notes. Photos are taken.

KRASIN	Have you started?

BORIS	Not yet.

Wrinkles and purplish stain over the frontal and parietal lobes. Skin has sunk roughly a centimetre in diameter where the skull has been opened to extract the brain…

Notes and photos. VLAD continues under:

KRASIN	Photographs?

BORIS	To prove what we did.

VLAD	…Tip of nose covered in dark pigments. Walls of nostril have become paper thin. Eyes half open and sinking in sockets…

BORIS	*(to KRASIN)* No one is allowed to enter until we are done.

VLAD	Lips now parted to reveal teeth.

BORIS	Not even Stalin.

VLAD	Brown spots on hands. Fingernails blue.

BORIS	This is science now. We must have peace.

One last photo.

The technicians fade away.

VLAD   Complete. Thank you.

KRASIN   All the best. Comrades.

KRASIN leaves.

NADIA 3 hovers.

VLAD   Did you get everything down?

NADIA 3   Yes.

She hands VLAD the notebook.

VLAD   Thank you. I…

She kisses him Russian style: three times on opposing cheeks.

She closes the door.

The embalmers alone with the body and LENIN himself.

BORIS pours a shot, his hand shaking.

BORIS   …Drink?

VLAD looks at the drink.

VLAD   No.

BORIS downs it like it's his last.

They stare at LENIN. He leaves.

BORIS   Vlad, I'm…

VLAD   Don't worry.

        They stare at the body.

        The body: it will tell us what to do.

***

        The embalming: perhaps realistic, perhaps not.

        Perhaps partially narrated. Perhaps silent.

        No matter what, it is a slow, scientific ritual.

        Precise as a dance.

        Formal as a catechism.

        Seamless as a ceremony.

        The music/sound is a haunted memory.

        VLAD leads. BORIS assists.

        After each section VLAD makes notes.

***

        The men don gowns.

        BORIS hands VLAD tools.

        VLAD's hands shake.

        He severs the sutures.

VLAD works on the body as BORIS begins dipping wool in chemicals.

It has begun.

***

Time passes.

Above: a GUARD, cold.

***

VLAD with an organ.

He places it in a jar.

As BORIS wraps the face with wet wool.

A healing.

***

The bath arrives.

They pour chemicals into buckets.

Steam.

Coughing, retching, blinking.

Both men hold cloths to their mouth and nose.

They lower the body gently into the bath.

A baptism.

***

Time passes.

The Guard watches as Nadia 3 enters with food.

She hands a basket to the Guard.

He takes it and leaves.

***

Boris and Vlad, resting.

The basket and a Thermos.

Vlad checks the body.

He is horrified.

The body is a terrible colour.

Boris grabs a scalpel.

Vlad takes it from him.

A moment of hesitation, then Vlad dives his hands into the chemicals.

Pain.

He makes small cuts.

Removes his burned hands.

Boris flushes them with water.

They watch the body.

They watch.

And watch.

And watch.

***

Time passes.

The GUARD *is approached by* KRASIN *carrying a letter.*

***

*V*LAD*, asleep.*

*B*ORIS *crumples the letter.*

He checks the body.

He wakes V*LAD.*

They stare down into the bath.

They clasp each other.

They raise the body from the bath.

*B*ORIS*, as if a tailor.*

He takes needle and thread.

And begins on the face. The body his canvas.

VLAD dabs the face and hands with cloth.

Life returning.

***

Time passes.

The mausoleum transformed.

VLAD and BORIS watch as: the sarcophagus arrives.

KRASIN and STALIN watch as NADIA 1 enters in mourning attire.

She steps forward.

LENIN is revealed: the body become symbol.

He is a work of art.

NADIA 1, unbelieving.

She weeps.

BORIS and VLAD.

As if a portrait.

On their faces: a marriage of exhaustion, relief, pity, pride.

LENIN slowly rises, moving and magical.

LENIN holds NADIA 1, comforts her.

NADIA 1   Oh Ilych, don't leave me, don't…

LENIN   Shhh…
           It's all right now.
           It's all right.

           The joke's on me.

                He looks to STALIN.

           It's on me.

                End of Act One.

ACT TWO

ENSEMBLE	1925.
	We—are Russians.
	No.
	Soviets.
	Yes.
	Soviets.
	A line of PEASANTS.
	LENIN, in the line himself.
LENIN	In Red Square, a long line of peasants snakes to the mausoleum.
PEASANT 1	Why do they keep a guard at Lenin's tomb?

PEASANT 2	You know what they say: Lenin lived, Lenin is alive, Lenin lives forever.
PEASANT 1	So why the guard?
PEASANT 2	What if he tries to escape!?

They laugh. They are hushed by the ENSEMBLE.

LENIN looks to STALIN,

LENIN	If only I could… Escape.

***

STALIN stares out a window.

KRASIN hovers.

STALIN	Look at that. Look at that…
KRASIN	Line?
STALIN	That LINE! They wait for…
KRASIN	Hours.
STALIN	Hours.
KRASIN	Days.
STALIN	Days.
KRASIN	Weeks.
STALIN	Weeks to see him.

KRASIN	Yes.
STALIN	Sadness.
KRASIN	Tears.
STALIN	Grief.

He turns from the window.

Take a note:

KRASIN writes.

"From now on, all citizens will refer to me as 'Father.'"
"Mother Russia and Father Stalin." It has a nice…

KRASIN	Ring?
STALIN	Ring to it. Now go. Wait. We must do something.
KRASIN	About…?
STALIN	Trotsky.
KRASIN	He is in exile.
STALIN	I know that.
KRASIN	In Mexico.
STALIN	I KNOW THAT! When Trotsky discovers that I have turned Lenin into a GOD, do you think HE won't want to be a god? Do you think HE won't want to

be HOLY? No, his vanity, his arrogance, his, his JEWY-NESS knows no BOUNDS. Who is our man in Mexico?

KRASIN   Ramon Mercader.

STALIN   Send a telegram.

           KRASIN writes.

           "Ramon. Stop.
           Buy ice pick. Stop.
           Find Trotsky. Stop.
           Kill Trotsky with ice pick. Stop."

           Read that back.

KRASIN   Ramon. Buy ice pick. Find Trotsky. Kill Trotsky with ice pick.

STALIN   Add: "Reward awaits. Stop.

           Your Father. Stalin."

                 ***

           BORIS's apartment. BORIS writes. NADIA 2 enters in a fur coat.

NADIA 2   The whole apartment is painted.

BORIS   Excellent.

NADIA 2   The new furniture arrives tomorrow.

BORIS   Wonderful.

NADIA 2	And what do you think of this!
BORIS	Lovely.
NADIA 2	You haven't looked!
BORIS	I'm sure it's—
NADIA 2	YOU'RE NOT PAYING ATTENTION, PAY ATTENTION!

BORIS turns.

| BORIS | Beautiful. Better? |

She smiles.

NADIA 2	And what will you do now?
BORIS	Now?
NADIA 2	You are a great scientist. What will you DO?
BORIS	What all great scientists do. Become an inspiration to humanity.
NADIA 2	Ah!
BORIS	Share my incredible life with those less fortunate and provide insight into the human condition.
NADIA 2	Naturally.
BORIS	And write my memoirs.
NADIA 2	Your memoirs?
BORIS	To be published only after my death.

NADIA 2   But wouldn't you make more money if—

BORIS   No, no, there is sensitive information here. *(his journal)* About my past. It must be published posthumously. Agreed?

NADIA 2   Do you mention me?

BORIS   A whole chapter!

NADIA 2   Just one?

BORIS   Ha!

                    She gives a lazy stretch.

NADIA 2   We should hire a maid.

BORIS   We'll see.

NADIA 2   We should have a *dacha* in the country…

BORIS   One thing at a time.

NADIA 2   We should buy some horses.

BORIS   …now, now, let's not…

NADIA 2   *(flirting)* And take lovers. You won't mind? If I took a lover—just for a little while?

                    She is behind him, kissing his neck.

BORIS   Perhaps… TWO whole chapters.

                    They kiss as she peeks at the pages.

***

VLAD   …And finally: "The Science of Death."

                *NADIA 3 works the slides. Perhaps they are images
                of dead people.*

                Necrobiosis is the death of individual cells, which
                are replaced with new ones. But, when an entire organ
                dies…

NADIA 3   Slide!

                Another slide.

VLAD   Necrosis or infarction occurs. An entire organ
                cannot replace itself, and soon…

NADIA 3   Slide!

                Slide.

VLAD   Clinical death takes hold: no breathing, no circu-
                lation, no neural activity. After several minutes of
                oxygen deprivation, the body moves to…

NADIA 3   Slide!

                Slide.

VLAD   Brain death. Once the brain goes, the heart doesn't
                know how to pump and the lungs don't know how
                to breathe and eventually…

NADIA 3   Slide!

Slide.

VLAD Somatic death occurs. The final, permanent, irreversible death of us all.

Unless, of course, one can preserve these cells for an extended period of time. Which is what I, Vladimir Davidovich Vorobiov, famously proved with the embalming of Lenin.

STUDENTS *(keen)* Professor, professor!

VLAD Yes?

STUDENT 1 What will you do now?

VLAD Now?

STUDENT 2 What will you do next?

VLAD What all great scientists do—share my knowledge with inferior students like you.

STUDENT 1 Will you share the secrets of Lenin's embalming?

VLAD Of course not.

STUDENT 1 What about Zbarsky?

VLAD What about him?

STUDENT 2 He's the toast of Moscow!

STUDENT 1 He's the king of Red Square!

STUDENT 2 He gets into any restaurant he wants!

STUDENT 1   Aren't you jealous?

A beat.

VLAD   *(fuming)* I am a man of SCIENCE, not society. Now
             go study my brilliance. Go!

They leave

NADIA 3 approaches.

NADIA 3   Does that include me?

VLAD   What's that?

NADIA 3   Am I… an inferior student? Like them?

VLAD is surprised.

VLAD   Oh no, no…

NADIA 3   Because I too want to learn. I too want to discover.
             I too want to be great.

VLAD looks at her.

VLAD   Pack your things.

Her jaw drops.

A vacation. To Moscow.

NADIA 3   *(shock)* …Oh…

He pours two shots of vodka, gives her one.

VLAD   The best champagne and the best caviar and the
              best hotel room overlooking Red Square.

              She is touched.

              You will be great. You will.

              He lifts his glass, and downs it.

                            ***

              LENIN and two PEASANTS.

              Two other PEASANTS watch.

LENIN   Two peasants are watching a parade.

PEASANT 1   *(whispers)* What's the difference between Lenin and
              Stalin?

LENIN   Says the one.

PEASANT 2   I don't know…

LENIN   Says the other.

PEASANT 2   …What?

PEASANT 1   Lenin collects the jokes that people tell about him.

PEASANT 2   And Stalin?

PEASANT 1   Collects the PEOPLE who tell jokes about him.

              They laugh.

The other PEASANTS reveal themselves to be STALIN and KRASIN.

STALIN   Comrades!

PEASANT 2   It was him! He told it, not me, not me!

PEASANT 1   No, no!

PEASANT 1 is dragged away.

LENIN   *(to STALIN)* This can't go on.

***

BORIS, VLAD and KRASIN.

KRASIN   Borislav Gerhardovich!

BORIS   Alexander Petrolovich!

KRASIN   How is our dear Nadia?

BORIS   Oy.

KRASIN   Success can be as difficult as poverty.

BORIS   I'll say.

KRASIN   And how is our good professor from the steppe?

VLAD   Can we get on with it? I have tickets to the Bolshoi.

KRASIN   Gentlemen: Stalin is very happy with your work.

BORIS   Send our thank yous, Sasha.

KRASIN   But…

BORIS   Yes?

KRASIN   It's been six months. The body. It has begun to, how
          shall I put it…

VLAD   Rot?

KRASIN   Something must be done.

BORIS   We warned you of this. The first embalming would
          not last forever.

KRASIN   Of course, but—

BORIS   We may have to re-embalm him.

KRASIN   I see.

BORIS   This will take time. And a number of other things
          Vladimir Davidovich and I will… need.

          Boris hands Krasin a paper.

KRASIN   Ten thousand rubles each?

BORIS   Naturally, we need to be paid.

KRASIN   A senior position in the Communist Party of Moscow?

BORIS   For me. It would help us enormously with…
          fundraising.

KRASIN   A lifetime appointment at the university?

BORIS   For Vladimir.

> *KRASIN considers.*

KRASIN   Well. I can see to the payment, and the party position, but…

I have no power over the university.

VLAD   I'm sorry?

BORIS   Surely it is deserved.

KRASIN   Perhaps, but—

VLAD   PERHAPS?

BORIS   Vlad.

KRASIN   But I am only prepared to grant you the first two.

VLAD   Is that so.
Well.
Add THIS to your list.
A dacha on the Black Sea.

KRASIN   What?

VLAD   A private apartment in Moscow.

KRASIN   Excuse me?

VLAD   My own private CHEF. SHALL I GO ON?

KRASIN   *(steamed)* And how do these things possibly relate to Lenin's body?

VLAD   They are critical for contemplating better methods of embalming.

KRASIN	You are playing a very dangerous game.
VLAD	No, I have already PLAYED the dangerous game.
BORIS	Vlad.
VLAD	You can't do this without me.
BORIS	Vlad.
VLAD	And now you have the gall to NEGOTIATE?!
BORIS	VLAD!

VLAD is silent.

Sasha. If you find others who can do the embalming for less, by all means, proceed. But these are… OUR… requirements.

KRASIN stares at them.

KRASIN	I'll be back in a minute.

He leaves.

BORIS	You've been drinking.
VLAD	I WANT MY FULL PROFESSORSHIP!
BORIS	I am getting us what we WANT!
VLAD	No, you're getting us what YOU want!
BORIS	This is a negotiation, there's got to be give and take.
VLAD	Nothing's changed, it's always about YOU.

BORIS   This part is MY job. Remember?

                 KRASIN returns.

KRASIN   Begin at once.

                           ***

                 Mexico. TROTSKY writing.

                 A knock on the door.

TROTSKY   ¿Si?

                 RAMON with ice pick.

RAMON   Comrade Trotsky.

TROTSKY   ¿Quién son usted? *(Who are you?)*

RAMON   Ramon Mercador.

TROTSKY   ¿Qué usted quiere? *(What do you want?)*

RAMON   A message—from Father Stalin.

                 He pins TROTSKY down. The ice pick looms.

TROTSKY   Nyet!

RAMON   "No habra' embalsamiento para usted, ah?" *There will be no embalming for you!*

                 The ice pick falls.

                           ***

The mausoleum.

VLAD enters with NADIA 3.

BORIS working on the body.

BORIS   What's she doing here? Get her out.

VLAD   Now, now, there's no reason—

BORIS   There's plenty of reasons.

VLAD   She has done a great deal for us.

BORIS   She knows too much already.

VLAD   She is now part of the staff.

BORIS   …What? We didn't discuss this.

VLAD   This part is MY job, remember?

             BORIS leaves.

             Come closer.
             Come.
             You see?

NADIA 3   Beautiful.

             VLAD takes a jar of embalming alcohol.

VLAD   Drink?

NADIA 3   Isn't that…?

VLAD   It's better. It's pure. And it's free.

NADIA 3   Why do you drink? Why? When you have—

VLAD   Shhh. Touch.

                 She stares.

                 Touch.

                 She touches LENIN.

                 We all die. And no matter who we are, no matter
                 what our problems, no matter what our fears, the
                 science is the same. It's all… chemistry.

                 (a seduction) Algor mortis: the body cools and the
                 eyes cloud over. Like milk.

                 Livor mortis. The blood clots and settles. The skin
                 turns blue and the face loses its life. A death mask.

                 Rigor mortis. Actin and myosin stiffen the muscles.
                 Like hardwood.

                 Autolysis. Microbes break down the blood, rupture
                 the intestines, breach the internal organs. Enzymes
                 eat the tissues, feasting on an internal banquet.

                 Putrefaction. The skin sours with streaks of black.
                 Gasses, swelling, and the smell of death.

                 And last, the body collapses. Dries itself out. Ashes
                 to ashes. Dust to dust.

                 This is death.

                 And this—have I halted.
                 This—have I prevented.

This—have I defeated.

NADIA 3   I want to know.

VLAD   Do you?

NADIA 3   I want to defeat death too.

VLAD   The secrets are all here. *(his head)*

And here.

He hands her the notebook.

They stare at LENIN.

NADIA 3   …Beautiful.

VLAD   Yes… Beautiful.

They kiss.

***

STALIN, staring out the window.

KRASIN enters with a telegram.

KRASIN   *(cautious)* Father Stalin.

STALIN   A year.

KRASIN   News.

STALIN   A year, and STILL they wait.

KRASIN   A telegram.

STALIN	Rain. Snow. Heat. And STILL they wait.
KRASIN	From Ramon Mercador. Trotsky. He's dead.

STALIN looks at KRASIN.

STALIN	No.
KRASIN	Yes.
STALIN	The ice pick?
KRASIN	Yes.
STALIN	In his head?
KRASIN	I'm not sure, but I assume…

STALIN takes a sharp intake of breath.

STALIN	*(moved)* Oh. Oh my. I am… I am the only one. Me.

We must celebrate. Take a note:

KRASIN writes.

"Create new medal."

KRASIN	For whom?
STALIN	The embalmers.

KRASIN	But they have already been paid a substantial—
STALIN	Create the award.
KRASIN	I am concerned, Father Stalin, the embalmers are becoming too—
STALIN	DO YOU SEE THAT LINE? DO YOU?

You want people lining up for YOU, don't you? You want them to wait for YOU, don't you? Wailing, crying, KEENING, wishing you back one more day, one more hour, one more SECOND, wishing you would live forever, forever, FOR-EV-ER. DON'T YOU?

KRASIN, sweating.

KRASIN	What, what kind of medal?
STALIN	I don't know... Something shiny. They're Jews. They'll like that.

***

The banquet.

Very Russian: grand, over the top.

All the ENSEMBLE present.

BORIS	Alexander Petrolovich!
KRASIN	Shh.
BORIS	What's wrong?

KRASIN   Did you know Trotsky?

BORIS   What?

KRASIN   Did you support Trotsky?

BORIS   Sasha, what's the matter?

KRASIN   Because if you did—

              VLAD enters, totally smashed.

VLAD   *(sings)* "Coachman, don't rush the horses…"

              Borislav Gerhardovich! I love you, you know that. *(to KRASIN, of BORIS)* I LOVE THIS MAN! Even when he wouldn't share his rations at university, even then…

              He spills his drink on KRASIN.

              Ooops.

KRASIN   Good God.

BORIS   The most important day of our lives, and you're drunk!

KRASIN   Ah, comrades!

              The APPARATCHIKS approach. APPARATCHIK 2 is hungover, but not drunk.

APPARAT 1   Comrades.

APPARAT 2   Comrades.

BORIS   Comrades.

Vlad	Comraaaaaades.
Apparat 2	Congratulations.
Boris	Thank you.
Apparat 1	And how is our good professor from the steppe?
Vlad	Who wants to know?
Boris	*(a save)* Thank you, comrades, for everything the committee has done for us.
Vlad	*(bowing)* Thank you, thank you, thank you.
Apparat 2	And what NEW miracles of science can we look forward to?
Boris	I am working on some… writing.
Apparat 1	"Writing"!
Apparat 2	First a scientist, then a hero, now a "writer"!
Vlad	He's a GENIUS.
Apparat 1	And will you reveal all your "secrets" in this "writing"?
Vlad	None about you, "comrades."
Apparat 2	Is that right?
Vlad	He only writes about things that are IMPORTANT.
Apparat 1	Is that so?
Apparat 2	Well then, you had best be careful what you write.

APPARAT 1	You don't want to end up like Trotsky.
BORIS	Trotsky?
VLAD	*(spits)* Trotsky!
APPARAT 1	Murdered.
APPARAT 2	Mexico.
APPARAT 1	Ice pick.
APPARAT 2	Head.
BORIS	What?
VLAD	TRAITOR!
APPARAT 1	Indeed.
KRASIN	Comrades, may I introduce you to a very dear friend? *(to BORIS)* Do something.

KRASIN and the APPARATCHIKS leave.

BORIS	Keep your mouth shut!
VLAD	Who will challenge us, Boris, WHO?
BORIS	This is POLITICS, remember?
VLAD	Politics don't matter anymore.
BORIS	Is that right?
VLAD	The power is in the science.

BORIS	These people are important.
VLAD	They're fools. Like you.
APPARAT 1	Ladies and gentlemen! Our national anthem.

All stand at attention.

The last bits of the Internationale plays.

VLAD sings louder than most.

STALIN enters, LENIN behind him.

ALL	(sing) 'Tis the final conflict Let each stand in his place. The international soviet Shall be the human race 'Tis the final conflict Let each stand in his place. The international working class Shall be the human race.
APPARAT 1	Long live Father Stalin, leader of the oppressed throughout the world!
ALL	Long Live Father Stalin!
STALIN	Comrades Vorobiov and Zbarsky.

They rise.

You have done a great thing. You have amazed scientists around the world. You have made our great leader Vladimir Iliych Lenin live forever. As he himself said:

LENIN/STALIN   "Sometimes… History needs a push."

STALIN   Come, accept your awards.

KRASIN   Borislav Gerhardovich Zbarsky.

> *Applause.*
>
> *STALIN places the award around BORIS's neck.*
>
> *They shake hands.*
>
> *Then: they kiss in standard Russian style—three times on apposing cheeks.*
>
> *Applause.*

Vladimir Davidovich Vorobiov.

> *VLAD goes up, wavering.*
>
> *STALIN drapes it on him.*
>
> *They shake hands.*
>
> *They kiss three times.*
>
> *And then: he kisses STALIN on the lips, joyous.*
>
> *A gasp from all.*
>
> *Everyone frozen.*
>
> *Then: STALIN smiles, tight and awkward.*
>
> *It gives way to a forced, horrible, inhuman, barking laugh.*

All laugh, forced.

Finally:

STALIN   To the reception!

A cheer.

All leave, except:

STALIN and KRASIN on one side. VLAD and BORIS on the other.

STALIN wipes his mouth, disgusted.

What do we know?

KRASIN   You mean…?

STALIN   What do we KNOW? About these "men."

KRASIN   I…

STALIN   Find out everything.

KRASIN   Of course.

STALIN   EVERYTHING.

KRASIN hustles after STALIN.

BORIS   What have you done?

VLAD   *(rapture)* I kissed Stalin. I did. Me.

BORIS   Have you gone completely mad?

VLAD   Jealous, Borislav Gerhardovich?

        Boris is agog.

BORIS   Listen to me. I will let you drink yourself to death.
        And I will let you throw your career away. But I will
        NOT let you take me down with you.

VLAD   It's me they need.

BORIS   Is that so?

VLAD   You couldn't embalm a cat.

BORIS   Is that right?

        VLAD grabs BORIS, drunk but violent.

VLAD   You won't take it away, not this time.

        BORIS pulls away.

BORIS   I don't want to be seen with you in public ever
        again. Is that understood?

                            ***

        STALIN and KRASIN.

        BORIS arrives.

STALIN Ah! Come in, come in.

BORIS   Father Stalin.

STALIN I was just looking at…

KRASIN   The file.

STALIN   The file.

BORIS   On...?

STALIN   You.

              Pause.

              It has come to my attention that you supported Trotsky
              during the revolution.

BORIS   ...I knew of him of course...

STALIN   Because he was a Jew.

BORIS   *(a glance to KRASIN)* ...Yes.

STALIN   And this is why you supported him?

BORIS   No, no...

STALIN   You didn't support a fellow Jew?

BORIS   No, no, I mean...

STALIN   You didn't support him at all.

BORIS   No.

STALIN   Really? Because...

              Comrade Trotsky was, as you know, a dear friend of
              our Great Leader. He was a founding revolutionary
              of this country. He was brutally murdered in Mexico.
              And you say, you did NOT support him?

Pause.

Now the tsar, he, HE was a traitor. Wasn't he?

Pause.

Were YOU a tsarist, Zbarsky?

BORIS   No.

STALIN   And yet you were not a Trotskyite?

Pause.

Ah! You were NEUTRAL… yes?

BORIS   Yes.

STALIN   But your colleague, your… queer friend Vorobiov…
             who did he support?

Pause.

Because a Trotskyite… I can forgive that. But a TSARIST?

BORIS   I don't know.

STALIN   Really. Classmates, scientists, Jews. And you didn't
             know who he supported?

Pause.

Come now, comrade.

KRASIN   You would be serving Mother Russia.

STALIN   And helping Her People.

KRASIN   And doing a Great Service.

STALIN   If you told us.

            BORIS thinks.

BORIS   No.

STALIN   No what?

BORIS   He was not a tsarist.

            STALIN looks at him.

STALIN   Really.

BORIS   No.

            STALIN looks at him.

STALIN   Well then.

            That will be all.
            Wait.
            It will soon be time for another embalming, yes?

BORIS   Yes.

STALIN   Don't fail me, Borislav Gerhardovich.

            BORIS nods slightly.

            Then leaves.

            Why do they lie?

KRASIN   Father Stalin…

STALIN	It makes them so much easier to KILL.
KRASIN	We need them.
STALIN	Do we?
KRASIN	Yes.
STALIN	Both of them?
KRASIN	I…
STALIN	Who is more important?
KRASIN	I…
STALIN	Who.
KRASIN	…Vorobiov.
STALIN	*(sighs)* How unfortunate.
KRASIN	…Yes.
STALIN	Find him. But don't… you know. Not yet. Not. Yet.

***

Vlad's office.

*Vlad and Nadia 3 looking at the embalming
notes.*

| VLAD | Very good, very good! You're learning quickly. |

NADIA 3   But after you immersed him in the bath…

VLAD   What?

NADIA 3   I can't quite make out what you've written here.

>   *APPARATCHIK1 bursts in. He has AGENT 2 with him.*

>   *VLAD hides the notebook.*

>   *The AGENT and APPARATCHIK are cool, calm and matter-of-fact throughout.*

VLAD   Excuse me!

APPARAT 1   We are from the Soviet Committee for Education Reformation.

VLAD   I am preparing a lecture!

APPARAT 1   We are here to inform you that from this day forward, there is no longer a chemistry department at this university.

VLAD   WHAT?

AGENT 2   "Chemistry" has been deemed of no value to the construction of the communist state.

APPARAT 1   From this day forward there is only a department for the "Practical Development of Electricity."

AGENT 2   And your "position" here has been eliminated.

>   *Pause.*

VLAD   *(to NADIA 3)* Tell my students I'll be late.

             She leaves.

             DO YOU KNOW WHO I AM?

APPARAT 1   Here is the order.

AGENT 2   Signed by Father Stalin himself.

             VLAD looks at it. Then:

VLAD   I will teach biology.

APPARAT 1   That department has too been reformed.

AGENT 2   There is only "The Department for Soviet Genetics."

VLAD   Entomology.

APPARAT 1   "The Battle Against Parasites."

VLAD   Zoology.

AGENT 2   "The Science of Hunting."

VLAD   THIS IS MADNESS!

APPARAT 1   No university will hire you.

AGENT 2   No one will ask for you.

APPARAT 1   No one will want you.

AGENT 2   There is nowhere for you to go, Professor.

APPARAT 1   Nowhere.

AGENT 2	You are doomed.
VLAD	Why are you doing this?

The agents move in: casually, quietly.

APPARAT 1	Your friend.
AGENT 2	Zbarsky.
APPARAT 1	Says you supported the tsar.
VLAD	…What?
AGENT 2	That's what he said.
APPARAT 1	Is it true?
AGENT 2	Is it?
VLAD	No, no, how could I, how could I support that, that dictator who, who murdered thousands of, of…
APPARAT 1	Jews?
AGENT 2	How could you have?
VLAD	How could I have.
AGENT 2	Supporting the tsar is, after all, a crime.
APPARAT 1	Punishable by death.
AGENT 2	Death, yes.
VLAD	…He, would, he would never…

AGENT 2   Never what?

APPARAT 1   Betray you?

                 VLAD looks at them.

                 There is a rumour.

AGENT 2   That your friend.

APPARAT 1   Zbarsky.

AGENT 2   Supported Trotsky.

APPARAT 1   Is that true?

VLAD   …I don't know, I…

APPARAT 1   Did HE support the tsar?

VLAD   No, no!

AGENT 2   And yet he didn't support Trotsky?

VLAD   …I don't know.

APPARAT 1   Classmates, scientists, Jews, and yet you didn't know
                 who he supported?

                 Silence.

                 Well.

AGENT 2   Then we have no choice but to believe Zbarsky.

APPARAT 1   And that would be so very unfortunate.

AGENT 2   But if we were to believe YOU, then I think…

APPARAT 1   We could leave here quite happy.

AGENT 2   Quite happy, yes.

APPARAT 1   Who should we believe…?

AGENT 2   Good professor from the steppe.

               VLAD struggles.

               He takes a bottle.

VLAD   A bottle of the finest?

APPARAT 1   No thank you.

AGENT 2   Never on the job.

               VLAD pours, his hands shaking.

               He drinks.

               Then.

VLAD   Yes.

APPARAT 1   Zbarsky knew Trotsky?

               VLAD nods his head.

               Zbarsky supported him?

               VLAD nods his head.

               Zbarsky is a traitor?

VLAD hesitates. Then:

VLAD   …Yes.

AGENT 2   Well.

APPARAT 1   That wasn't so hard, was it?

AGENT 2   Now.

APPARAT 1   Your keys.

VLAD   Keys?

AGENT 2   To the mausoleum.

VLAD   …What?

APPARAT 1   And then off to prison.

AGENT 2   You are under arrest.

VLAD   But you said…!

APPARAT 1   NOW!

AGENT 2 pulls out a gun.

My comrade isn't so steady with a gun.

AGENT 2 places the gun to VLAD's head.

He laughs and laughs.

VLAD slowly hands over the keys.

***

Boris's apartment

BORIS   Nadia, have you seen my memoir?

NADIA 2   I'm going out.

BORIS   You're not meeting a LOVER, are you?

NADIA 2   And if I was?

BORIS   It doesn't look good, it doesn't help with my stand-ing in the party!

NADIA 2   EVERYONE in the party has a lover, Boris.

BORIS   Where the devil is my memoir?

          APPARATCHIK 2 bursts in with AGENT 1. They are calm, cool and matter-of-fact.

APPARAT 2 Zbarsky.

BORIS   What do you want?

AGENT 1   Come with us.

BORIS   Where?

APPARAT 2 None of your concern.

BORIS   Why?

AGENT 1   None of your concern

          They bind him.

BORIS   Nadia! Call Krasin, call Vorobiov, tell him—

AGENT 1   They can't help you, Zbarsky.

APPARAT 2   No one can.

AGENT 1   You are doomed.

> *AGENT 1 drags him off.*
>
> *Then: NADIA 2 hands the APPARATCHIK the memoir.*
>
> *The AGENT pulls her in. He kisses her, the betrayal sealed.*

***

> *KRASIN, surprised to see STALIN with APPARAT-CHIK 2.*
>
> *LENIN hovers.*

STALIN   Ah! Come in, come in.

KRASIN   Comrade.

APPARAT 2   Comrade.

STALIN   I was just looking at...

APPARAT 2   The file.

STALIN   The file.

KRASIN   On...?

STALIN   You.

Pause.

I asked you for EVERYTHING.

Pause.

But it has been brought to my attention:

APPARAT 2	The memoir.
STALIN	The memoir. Written by…
APPARAT 2	Your friend…
STALIN	Your FRIEND…
APPARAT 2	Zbarsky.
STALIN	Detailing…
APPARAT 2	His support of Trotsky.
STALIN	Your FRIEND.
KRASIN	But, Father Stalin, I…
STALIN	He was your FRIEND, was he not? He must be, because on—
APPARAT 2	Page thirty-eight.
STALIN	Page thirty-eight, read it.
APPARAT 2	"My good friend Krasin, who got me the job at the chemical plant."

STALIN	"My good FRIEND," "My GOOD friend," "MY GOOD FRIEND."
KRASIN	I…
STALIN	Zbarsky is a TRAITOR and you are his FRIEND?

> *Silence.*

Are you?

> *Silence.*

Take a note.

> *KRASIN takes out a pad, hand shaking.*

To all agents.

"Find Krasin.
Send him to Northern Gulag.
Your father, Stalin."

Read that back.

KRASIN	*(trembling)* "Find… find Krasin. Send him to Northern Gulag. Your father, Stalin."
STALIN	Now go.

> *KRASIN steps away.*

(to APPARATCHIK 2) He always did believe in freezing.

> *APPARATCHIK 2 laughs, and leaves.*

KRASIN   *(to audience)* It was then that I died.

        KRASIN leaves.

STALIN   *(to audience)* I, on the other hand, did not die until 1953.

LENIN   I know.

STALIN   *(pleased)* I had MYSELF embalmed. To lay next to you for all time.

LENIN   Until Khrushchev put you where you belong.

STALIN   Where's that?

LENIN   In the ground.

STALIN   Really?

LENIN   Yes.

STALIN   Was there sadness?

LENIN   Oh ho!

STALIN   Tears?

LENIN   Of a kind.

STALIN   Grief?

LENIN   …For an eternity.

        ***

VLAD in a prison cell.

The GUARD *enters with* BORIS.

GUARD   Vorobiov! You've got company.

BORIS is thrown in.

BORIS   *(whisper)* What's going on?

VLAD   I don't know.

BORIS   When did they get you?

VLAD   This morning.

BORIS   We need Krasin.

VLAD   Krasin is dead.

BORIS   What?

VLAD   They told me on the way here.

BORIS   My God…

VLAD   What are we going to do?

BORIS   You tell me.

VLAD   What do you mean?

BORIS   If it weren't for you, none of this would have happened.

VLAD   I knew from the start we shouldn't get messed up in this.

BORIS   I knew from the start I shouldn't have called for you.

VLAD   And now I am the friend of a traitor who was friends
            with a traitor.

            Boris looks at him.

BORIS   Did you… Did you tell them?

VLAD   About what?

BORIS   You did. Didn't you.

VLAD   I don't know what you're talking about.

BORIS   About Trotsky!

VLAD   No! Yes!

BORIS   What?!

VLAD   They told me YOU told them I supported the tsar!

BORIS   And you BELIEVED THEM?

VLAD   I… I…

BORIS   I DEFENDED you! I LIED for you! I told them you were
            INNOCENT!

VLAD   *(it sinks in)* Oh God…

BORIS   So, you told them, you told them I…?

VLAD   …Boris.

            *Boris attacks him. He drags VLAD down to the
            ground and starts to choke him.*

Boris!

BORIS   We had a chance, Vlad. We had a chance to survive. We had a chance to LIVE in this dead, damned,
decaying world. But no: you betray our beliefs. You
kiss away our calling. You drink us into a cold grave.
We are dead! Do you hear me? WE. ARE. DEAD.

VLAD is turning blue. BORIS lets go.

No. No. I hope you live FOREVER. I hope you never
stop rotting. Never.

VLAD is shaking.

VLAD   I'll tell them.

BORIS   It's too late.

VLAD   I'll confess.

BORIS   Too late.

GUARD   Vorobiov!

VLAD looks confused.

You're free to go.

VLAD   …Wha…?

GUARD   Come on.

VLAD is distraught.

He grabs for BORIS's hands.

VLAD	Boris, I won't leave you, I won't.
GUARD	MOVE IT!
VLAD	Boris!! BORIS!!!

BORIS turns away.

(in Hebrew) Slicha, Boris, *Slicha*! Forgive me.

VLAD is dragged off.

BORIS alone.

BORIS	*(to audience)* Am I the hero of this story? I think not.

***

NADIA 3, alone in VLAD's office.

VLAD arrives.

NADIA 3	Where have you been?
VLAD	Shh.
NADIA 3	What happened?
VLAD	Shh.

VLAD goes to his desk.

He finds a gun.

Hides it.

NADIA 3	What are you doing?

VLAD   *(whispers)* Have they come?

NADIA 3   Who?

VLAD   They're following me.

                VLAD takes out his notebook.

                They will be here soon. You must go.

NADIA 3   They won't take you.

VLAD   They will. They have.

NADIA 3   They need you.

VLAD   No. They need this.

                He hands her the notebook.

                Take it.

                The AGENTS arrive. She hides it.

AGENT 2   Citizen Vorobiov.

VLAD   "Citizen," now.

AGENT 2   We hear you've been sick.

VLAD   …Oh?

AGENT 1   We hear you have been having troubles with your—

AGENT 2   Liver.

VLAD   My liver?

AGENT 2	We hear you have been in great pain.
AGENT 1	We've made arrangements for you to see the doctor.
AGENT 2	Come with us.
AGENT 1	I am sure the doctor will "cure" you of your pain.
AGENT 2	Forever.
VLAD	Is that so?
AGENT 1	Unless…
AGENT 2	Unless…
AGENT 1	You give us what we need.
VLAD	And that is?
AGENT 1	You know.
AGENT 2	The notebook.

VLAD looks to NADIA.

VLAD	And if I don't?
NADIA 3	Vladimir!
AGENT 2	*(grabs NADIA 3)* Then she must die.
AGENT 1	*(a gun to her head)* Such a shame. To waste such beauty.
AGENT 2	And talent, to be sure.
AGENT 1	To be sure.

Vlad thinks.

He goes to the desk.

Grabs a plain notebook.

VLAD	Here. Here is what you want. Here. Ah! She goes first.
NADIA 3	Vladimir…
VLAD	Go. It will be better this way.

They let her go.

In tears, she leaves.

He hands over a notebook.

AGENT 1	This…
AGENT 2	These pages…
AGENT 1	This book is…
AGENT 2	BLANK!

VLAD begins to laugh.

He is laughing and crying.

VLAD	I am the hero. I am the real hero of this story!

He points at LENIN, *who is unseen by the* AGENTS:

See him?
He is because of me.
I made him live forever, ME.

He reveals the gun. They pull out theirs.

You won't bury me like the others.
I won't be left to rot in the open grave of history.
No, I will be the one to laugh! Me!

LENIN   Listen to this. This is a good one.

AGENT 1   Comrade!

LENIN   What did Vladimir Vorobiov say before committing
               suicide?

VLAD points the gun at his head.

AGENTS   Comrade!

VLAD   Comrades… don't… shoot!

VLAD laughs and cries until: a gunshot.

***

LENIN watches: a Gulag.

Cold.

Three PRISONERS huddle.

PRISONER 1   What are you in for?

PRISONER 2   I called Zbarsky a revolutionary.

PRISONER 1   *(bitter)* That's funny.

PRISONER 2   Why?

PRISONER 1   I called Zbarsky a counter-revolutionary.

PRISONER 3   That's funny.

PRISONER 2   Why?

> *BORIS shows his face.*

BORIS   I AM Zbarsky.

> *Silence, save for the wind.*

PRISONER 1   Do you think we'll die soon?

PRISONER 2   I don't know.

BORIS   I hope so.

> *Silence.*

I hope so.

> *Snow starts to fall.*

***

> *The present day bursts in: modern dress, modern music.*

ENSEMBLE   March.

2010.

Moscow.

LENIN I am Lenin.

I am not a myth.
I am not a god.
And I am not the hero of this story.

I am a simply a man
who never wanted to be kept alive
in a joke with no punchline.

> LENIN *looks at the modern world around him.*

Me? I could die today.
If only…
If only they'd stop waiting.

> LENIN *lies down in the sarcophagus.*

> *The* ENSEMBLE *line up.*

> *One by one, they pass by* LENIN's *corpse.*

> *The last are the embalmers.*

***

> *As the audience leave, perhaps they too pass by*
> LENIN.

> *Taking the story with them.*

> *Fin.*

PLAYWRIGHT'S NOTES

This play is a work of fiction. I am greatly indebted to the book *Lenin's Embalmers* by Ilya Zbarsky and Samuel Hutchinson, translated by Barbara Bray. Although I have altered timelines and combined characters for dramatic purposes, the basic story is historically accurate:

- Boris Zbarsky and Vladimir Vorobiov were chosen to embalm Vladimir Lenin after his death in 1924.

- The embalming—which took almost four months—was a scientific "miracle" at the time, and was much applauded by scientists around the world.

- Both Boris and Vlad reached levels of power and influence that ultimately led to their ends at the hands of a paranoid Stalinist regime.

- For a detailed look at their stories, read Zbarsky's book. I also recommend *Hammer & Tickle: A History of Communism Told Through Communist Jokes* by Ben Lewis for a look at Russian humour.

ACKNOWLEDGEMENTS

This play was written with the generous assistance of the following organizations and individuals: Ensemble Studio Theatre, Alfred P. Sloan Foundation, the Shaw Festival of Canada, the Stratford Shakespeare Festival of Canada, the Citadel Theatre New Play Program, Bob Baker, James MacDonald, Geoffrey Brumlik, Guido Tondino, Victoria Zimski, William Carden, Graeme Gillis, Carlos Ornesto, Linsay Firman, Dorothy Hutchins, Christine Ogden, Lauren Gunderson, Joanna Falck, Keira Loughran, Robert Blacker, Susie Moloney.

A special thanks to my embalming consultant Dorothy Hutchins. Not only did she pass on invaluable technical information, she also shared with me the passion, care, humanity, sanctity and dedication of her profession.

And thanks to my parents, who were both born in the Russian Ukraine in the 1920s. Both they—and my extended family—suffered first-hand under Stalin's ideology. Nevertheless, my parents laugh more than anyone I know.

photo by Nicholas Seiflow

Vern Thiessen is one of Canada's most-produced playwrights. His plays have been seen across Canada, the United States, Asia, the United Kingdom, the Middle East and Europe. Well-known works include *Vimy, Shakespeare's Will* and *Apple. Einstein's Gift, A More Perfect Union* and *Lenin's Embalmers* have all been seen off-Broadway. His plays for young audiences include *Bird Brain, Dawn Quixote* and *Windmill*. With composer/collaborator Olaf Pyttlik he has created two musicals, *Rich* and *Rapa Nui*. Thiessen is also the author of several adaptations, including *Wuthering Heights*. He is the winner of many awards including the Governor General's Literary Award, Canada's highest honour for playwriting. Thiessen is a past president of the Playwrights Guild of Canada and of the Writers Guild of Alberta. He splits his time between Canada and New York City.